feeling
saucy

feeling
saucy

SENSATIONAL HOMEMADE SAUCES TO STIR YOUR SENSES

Love Food ® is an imprint of Parragon Books Ltd

Parragon
Queen Street House
4 Queen Street
Bath BA1 1HE, UK

Copyright © Parragon Books Ltd 2007

Love Food ® and the accompanying heart device is a trademark of Parragon Books Ltd

Introduction by Lorraine Turner
Edited by Fiona Biggs
Designed by Emily Lewis and Sian Williams
Photography by Mike Cooper
Food Styling by Lincoln Jefferson

ISBN 978-1-4075-2709-3

Printed in China

NOTES FOR THE READER
This book uses imperial, metric, and US cup measurements. Follow the same units of
measurement throughout; do not mix metric and imperial. All spoon measurements are
level, unless otherwise stated: teaspoons are assumed to be 5 ml and tablespoons are
assumed to be 15 ml. Unless otherwise stated, milk is assumed to be semi-skimmed, eggs
and individual vegetables such as potatoes are medium, and pepper is freshly ground black
pepper. Sufferers from liver disease and those with weakened immune systems should never
eat raw fish. Recipes using raw or very lightly cooked eggs should be avoided by infants, the
elderly, pregnant women, convalescents, and anyone with a chronic condition. The times
given are an approximate guide only. Preparation times differ according to the techniques
used by different people and the cooking times may also vary from those given. Optional
ingredients, variations or serving suggestions have not been included in the calculations.

contents

introduction 6

main attraction 8

side show 30

dress to impress 52

sauce pot 74

index 96

introduction

Sauces are a wonderful invention: they enliven and elevate the humblest of dishes. Where there is blandness, they add excitement, not to mention a wonderful flavor and contrast in texture and color. They are an asset when entertaining as they can be made in advance and reheated before serving.

There is something about pouring a sauce at a dinner party that adds a touch of finesse to the occasion. A well-made sauce looks deceptively impressive, yet it is usually very easy to make. Although some sauces need little attention during cooking, they present no great challenge and are therefore ideal for the novice cook. Even if you are completely new to the kitchen, you will find the sauces in this book very simple to make and perfect to serve, whatever the occasion.

Sauces can be savory or sweet, hot or cold, and there are many different types, such as dipping sauces, pouring sauces, dressings, gravies, sauces for fillings (for use in dishes such as lasagna or pies), and dessert sauces.

Sauces can help to disguise different foods, and are therefore ideal for hoodwinking fussy children into eating vegetables and other foods that they may normally refuse to eat. They also add a welcome moistness to any dishes that are particularly dry.

So versatile

A single sauce may be a perfect partner for a variety of different dishes. For example, Satay Sauce makes a wonderful complement to stir-fried chicken, yet it is also good with vegetable kebabs or a variety of noodle dishes. Classic Bolognese Sauce is best known for its association with spaghetti, but it is also delicious as a filling for lasagna, in a potato-topped pie or on top of a baked potato. Gravy will partner a wide range of meals, not just roast meat, but also a range of savory pies, while desserts such as fruit pies, tarts, or baked fruit are practically queuing up to be matched with a rich chocolate sauce or that timeless old favorite, custard sauce.

Some sauces also serve as a base for other sauces: for example Béchamel Sauce is a tasty white sauce on its own, but you can add different ingredients to it to create new and exciting sauces. The addition of grated cheese, for instance, will transform a Béchamel Sauce into a mouthwatering cheese sauce. Or you can add some chopped fresh mixed herbs for a delightful herb sauce.

With inexpensive basic ingredients, most sauces are economical to make. You can always splash out on more expensive ingredients, such as wine and liqueurs, when your budget allows, but these are not essential. Generally you may well find that your homemade sauce works out a lot less expensive than a store-bought version, and you will have the added comfort of knowing that it is completely free of artificial additives.

Sauces can be healthy and nutritious too. A basic Béchamel Sauce, made predominantly with milk, is rich in protein and calcium, essential for good body-tissue formation and healthy muscles, teeth, and bones. The honey in a Honey & Yogurt Dressing doesn't just add sweetness, it has antibacterial properties too, while the yogurt is an aid to digestion, helping to preserve the balance of friendly flora in the digestive system.

For the health-conscious, the amount of saturated fat can be reduced by choosing lowfat versions of ingredients where possible. For example, opt for lowfat yogurt, skim or half-fat milk, and half-fat cheese and crème fraîche. The Slim-line Dressing in this book will give a low-cal lift to salads and sandwiches.

A good homemade sauce is very quick to make, but you can save even more time by making double quantities and chilling or freezing the remainder for another occasion.

Dressings and cold sauces are completely portable and excellent for picnics and lunch bags, but many other sauces can also be made in advance, transported somewhere else and then reheated—ideal for a barbecue or if you are taking a meal round to a friend or loved one.

Whatever the occasion, within the pages of this book you will find an impressive selection of tempting sauces just waiting for you to try them. Whether you are serving succulent roast lamb with a delicious Mint Sauce, a steaming plate of pasta with a Red Wine Sauce, or a fresh mixed salad with a Basil, Chive & Lemon Dressing, you are sure to impress your household and your guests with the irresistible colors and flavors of the sauces in this book. Many of the sauces are suitable for vegetarians too, so if you mix them with some freshly cooked grains or noodles, you will have a ready supply of wonderful dishes that any vegetarian will find hard to resist. And for dessert, what could start a stampede for the sauce boat more effectively than to fill it with a mouthwatering Chocolate Fudge Sauce or a tempting Maple Sauce, absolutely delicious when served with ice cream?

After you have sampled the sauces in this book, why not try making some creations of your own? You could use a plain sauce as a base, and then add extra ingredients and flavorings of your choice to provide a perfect complement to a particular dish. When you have mastered the basics of making the Fresh Tomato Sauce in this book, for instance, why not add some chopped fresh basil, or some canned lentils to make a more substantial and satisfying sauce that would be ideal served over pasta, freshly cooked rice, or a baked potato? The key is to experiment: simply by changing combinations of ingredients, or by varying the flavorings you use, you can transform the flavor, consistency, or color of a sauce into something quite different. So be brave and unleash your creativity!

And, for the person who has everything, some of the sauces in this book, such as Basil Pesto, Red Wine Sauce, Apple Sauce, Herb Vinaigrette, Orange Sauce, and Chocolate Brandy Sauce would make a great gift. Put the sauce in a really attractive jar, then add some pretty decorations and a label to personalize your gift.

main attraction

This chapter is brimming with inspirational sauces for satisfying main meals, light suppers, and lunch dishes that will delight everyone who tries them.

fresh tomato sauce

makes about 4 cups

1 tbsp olive oil

1 small onion, chopped

2–3 garlic cloves, crushed (optional)

1 small celery stalk, finely chopped

1 bay leaf

1 lb/450 g ripe tomatoes, peeled and chopped

1 tbsp tomato paste, blended with 5 fl oz/150 ml water

few sprigs fresh oregano

pepper

Heat the oil in a heavy-bottom pan, add the onion, garlic, if using, celery, and bay leaf, and gently sauté, stirring frequently, for 5 minutes.

Stir in the tomatoes with the blended tomato paste. Add pepper to taste and the oregano. Bring to a boil, then reduce the heat, cover, and simmer, stirring occasionally, for 20–25 minutes until the tomatoes have completely collapsed. If liked, simmer for an additional 20 minutes to give a thicker sauce.

Discard the bay leaf and the oregano. Transfer to a food processor and process to a chunky paste. If a smooth sauce is preferred, pass through a fine nonmetallic strainer. Taste and adjust the seasoning if necessary. Reheat and use as required.

classic bolognese meat sauce

serves 4

2 tbsp olive oil
1 tbsp butter
1 small onion, finely chopped
1 carrot, finely chopped
1 celery stalk, finely chopped
¾ cup mushrooms, diced
8 oz/225 g ground beef
2¾ oz/75 g lean bacon
  or ham, diced
2 chicken livers, chopped
2 tbsp tomato paste

½ cup dry white wine
½ tsp freshly grated nutmeg
1¼ cups chicken stock
4 fl oz/125 ml heavy cream
1 lb/450 g dried spaghetti
salt and pepper
2 tbsp chopped fresh parsley,
  to garnish
freshly grated Parmesan
  cheese, to serve

Heat the oil and butter in a large pan over medium heat. Add the onion, carrot, celery, and mushrooms to the pan, then fry until softened. Add the beef and bacon to the pan and fry until the beef is evenly browned.

Stir in the chicken livers and tomato paste and cook for 2–3 minutes. Pour in the wine and season with salt and pepper and the nutmeg. Add the stock. Bring to a boil, then cover and simmer gently over low heat for 1 hour. Stir in the cream and simmer, uncovered, until reduced.

Bring a large pan of lightly salted water to a boil, add the pasta, and cook until it is tender but still firm to the bite. Drain and transfer to a warmed serving dish.

Pour half the sauce over the pasta. Toss well to mix. Spoon the remaining sauce over the top. Garnish with the parsley and serve with the cheese.

arrabbiata sauce

makes about 2½ cups

2 tbsp olive oil

2 garlic cloves, chopped

1 fresh red serrano chile, seeded and chopped

1 tbsp grated lemon rind

1 lb/450 g ripe tomatoes, peeled and chopped

1 tbsp tomato paste, blended with ⅔ cup water

pinch of superfine sugar

1 tbsp balsamic vinegar

1 tbsp chopped fresh marjoram

pepper

Heat the oil in a heavy-bottom pan, add the garlic and chile and sauté, stirring continuously, for 1 minute. Sprinkle in the lemon rind and stir, then add the tomatoes with the blended tomato paste. Add the sugar and bring to a boil, then reduce the heat and simmer for 12 minutes.

Add the vinegar and marjoram and simmer for an additional 5 minutes. Add pepper to taste. Serve hot.

béchamel sauce

béarnaise sauce

béchamel sauce

makes about 1½ cups

1¼ cups milk
1 small onion, studded with 2–3 cloves
1 mace blade
1 fresh bay leaf
3–4 white or black peppercorns
1 small piece carrot, peeled
2 tbsp unsalted butter or margarine
¼ cup all-purpose flour
salt and pepper

Pour the milk into a small heavy-bottom pan with a lid. Add the onion, mace, bay leaf, peppercorns, and carrot. Heat over a gentle heat and slowly bring just to a boil. Remove from the heat, cover, and set aside for at least 30 minutes. Strain and reheat until warm.

Melt the butter in a separate small pan and sprinkle in the flour. Cook over gentle heat, stirring continuously with a wooden spoon, for 2 minutes. Remove from the heat and gradually stir in the warmed infused milk, adding a little at a time and stirring until the milk has been incorporated before adding more. When all the milk has been added, return to the heat and cook, stirring, until thick, smooth, and glossy. Add salt and pepper to taste and serve.

béarnaise sauce

makes about ½ cup

4 tbsp tarragon vinegar
1 shallot, finely chopped
2 egg yolks
6 tbsp butter, softened
salt and pepper

Put the vinegar and shallot into a small, heavy-bottom pan over low–medium heat and let simmer until reduced to 1 tablespoon. Let cool.

Strain the vinegar mixture into a heatproof bowl set over a pan of simmering water. Add the egg yolks and whisk together until thick. Gradually add the butter in small pieces, whisking after each addition, until combined and the sauce has thickened. Season to taste with salt and pepper and serve.

black bean sauce

makes about ⅔ cup

1 tbsp peanut oil
2 tbsp fermented black beans, finely chopped
1 garlic clove, chopped
1 tbsp grated fresh ginger
1 shallot, chopped
2 scallions, finely chopped
2 small fresh green chiles, seeded and chopped
1 tbsp light soy sauce
1 tbsp strained freshly squeezed lemon juice
⅔ cup vegetable stock
1–2 tsp superfine sugar, or to taste
salt and pepper

Heat a wok over high heat for 30 seconds.
Add the oil, swirl around to coat the bottom
of the wok, and heat for 30 seconds. Add the
black beans, garlic, ginger, and shallot and
stir-fry for 2 minutes.

Add the scallions and chiles and stir-fry for 3 minutes.
Add the soy sauce and lemon juice and simmer for
2 minutes. Add the stock and sugar with salt and
pepper to taste and simmer for an additional
2 minutes. Use as required.

hollandaise sauce

makes about 1 cup
2 tbsp white wine vinegar
1 tbsp water
2 egg yolks
4 oz/115 g unsalted butter, slightly softened
  and diced
lemon juice (optional)
salt and pepper

Pour the vinegar and water into a small
heavy-bottom pan and bring to a boil.
Boil for 3 minutes, or until reduced by half.
Remove from the heat and let cool slightly.

Put the egg yolks in a heatproof bowl and beat in
the cooled vinegar water. Set over a pan of gently
simmering water, ensuring that the base of
the bowl does not touch the simmering water.

Cook, stirring continuously with a wooden spoon,
until the mixture thickens slightly and lightly coats
the back of the spoon.

Keeping the water simmering, add the butter, a piece
at a time, until the sauce is thick, smooth, and glossy.
Add a little lemon juice if the mixture is too thick and
to give a more piquant flavor. Add salt and pepper to
taste and serve warm.

basil pesto

sun-dried tomato pesto

basil pesto

makes about 1 cup

1⅓ cups fresh basil leaves
1 garlic clove
¼ cup toasted pine nuts
½–⅔ cup extra virgin olive oil
¼ cup freshly grated Parmesan cheese
1–2 tsp freshly squeezed lemon juice
  (optional)
salt and pepper

Tear the basil leaves and put in a large mortar with the garlic, pine nuts, and 1 tablespoon of the oil. Pound with a pestle to form a paste.

Gradually work in the remaining oil to form a thick sauce. Add salt and pepper to taste and stir in the Parmesan cheese. If liked, slacken slightly with the lemon juice.

sun-dried tomato pesto

makes about 1 cup

¼ cup pine nuts
2 garlic cloves, coarsely chopped
8 oz/225 g sun-dried tomatoes in
  of the oil, drained and coarsely
  chopped
1 tsp coarse salt
¼ cup freshly grated Parmesan
  cheese
½–⅔ cup extra virgin olive oil

Dry-fry the pine nuts in a heavy-bottom skillet for 30–60 seconds, until golden. Remove from the skillet and let cool, then place in the food processor with the garlic, sun-dried tomatoes, and salt. Process to a paste. Add the Parmesan cheese and process briefly again. Then add ½ cup oil and process again. If the consistency is too thick, add the remaining oil and process again until smooth.

sweet & sour sauce

serves 4–6

3 tbsp white rice vinegar

2 tbsp sugar

1 tbsp light soy sauce

1 tbsp tomato ketchup

1½ tbsp vegetable or peanut oil

1 green bell pepper, roughly chopped

1 small onion, roughly chopped

1 small carrot, finely sliced

½ tsp finely chopped garlic

½ tsp finely chopped fresh ginger

⅔ cup pineapple chunks

Mix together the vinegar, sugar, soy sauce, and ketchup. Set aside.

In a preheated wok or deep pan, heat 1 tablespoon of the oil and stir-fry the bell pepper, onion, and carrot for 2 minutes. Remove and set aside.

In the clean preheated wok, heat the remaining oil and stir-fry the garlic and ginger until fragrant. Add the vinegar mixture. Bring back to a boil and add the pineapple chunks. Finally add the bell pepper, onion, and carrot. Stir until warmed through and serve immediately with stir-fried meat of your choice.

asparagus sauce

makes about 1¼ cups

⅔ cup chicken stock
1 bouquet garni, consisting of
   3 fresh parsley sprigs, 2 fresh
   thyme sprigs, 1 bay leaf, and a
   small celery stalk tied together
2 mushrooms, chopped
6 scallions, chopped

1 lb 9 oz/700 g green
   asparagus
3 tbsp butter
4 tbsp chopped fresh parsley
2 tbsp all-purpose flour
1 tbsp superfine sugar
salt and pepper

Put the chicken stock into a pan and add the bouquet garni, mushrooms, and 2 of the scallions. Bring to a boil, then reduce the heat, cover, and simmer gently for 20 minutes.

Meanwhile, cut off and discard the woody ends of the asparagus stems. Blanch in lightly salted boiling water for 2 minutes, then drain and refresh under cold water. Drain well again. Melt 2 tablespoons of the butter in a heavy-bottom skillet over medium heat. Add the asparagus, parsley, and remaining scallions and cook, stirring gently, for 5 minutes. Remove from the heat.

Using a fork, mash together the remaining butter and the flour to make a beurre manié paste. Remove and discard the bouquet garni from the chicken stock. Gradually stir in small pieces of the beurre manié until they are absorbed and the mixture is thickened. Remove from the heat and let cool slightly.

Transfer the asparagus mixture to the blender, add the sugar and 4 tablespoons of the stock mixture, and season with salt and pepper. Process to a smooth paste, adding stock mixture until you achieve the desired consistency. Stop and scrape down the sides as necessary. Taste and adjust the seasoning.

red wine sauce

makes about 1 cup
⅔ cup Gravy (see page 40)
4 tbsp red wine, such as a Burgundy
1 tbsp red currant jelly

Blend the Gravy with the wine and pour into a small heavy-bottom pan. Add the red currant jelly and warm over a gentle heat, stirring, until blended.

Bring to a boil, then reduce the heat and simmer for 2 minutes. Serve hot.

side show

Give a boost to snacks and accompaniments with the delicious sauces in this section. They are guaranteed to have everyone coming back for more.

cranberry sauce

makes about 2 cups

1 lb/450 g fresh or thawed frozen cranberries

1 tbsp grated orange rind, preferably unwaxed

⅔ cup freshly squeezed orange juice

½ cup soft light brown sugar

⅔ cup water

1–2 tbsp Cointreau (optional)

Put the cranberries in a heavy-bottom pan with the orange rind and juice, most of the sugar, and the water. Bring to a boil, then reduce the heat and simmer for 12–15 minutes, until the cranberries have burst.

Remove from the heat, taste, and add the remaining sugar, if liked, with the Cointreau, if using. Serve warm or cold.

horseradish sauce

serves 6–8

6 tbsp creamed horseradish sauce
6 tbsp sour cream

In a small serving bowl, mix the horseradish sauce and sour cream together. Serve the sauce with roast beef, or with smoked fish such as trout or mackerel.

mint sauce

makes about ½ cup
3 tbsp chopped fresh mint
2–3 tsp superfine sugar, or to taste
2 tbsp just-boiled water
3–4 tbsp white wine vinegar
   or malt vinegar

Put the mint in a small heatproof bowl and add
2 teaspoons of the sugar. Let the boiled water
cool for about 1 minute, then pour over the mint.
Stir until the sugar has dissolved, then set aside
to infuse for 10 minutes.

Add the vinegar to taste, cover, and leave to
stand for 1 hour. Stir and serve.

barbecue sauce

chile sauce

barbecue sauce

makes about 1 cup

1 tbsp olive oil

1 small onion, finely chopped

2–3 garlic cloves, crushed

1 fresh red jalapeño chile, seeded and
finely chopped (optional)

2 tsp tomato paste

1 tsp (or to taste) powdered mustard

1 tbsp red wine vinegar

1 tbsp Worcestershire sauce

2–3 tsp dark brown sugar

1¼ cups water

Heat the oil in a small heavy-bottom pan,
add the onion, garlic, and chile, if using,
and gently sauté, stirring frequently, for
3 minutes, or until beginning to soften.
Remove from the heat.

Blend together the tomato paste, mustard,
vinegar and Worcestershire sauce to make
a paste, then stir into the onion mixture
with 2 teaspoons of the sugar. Mix well,
then gradually stir in the water.

Return to the heat and bring to a boil,
stirring frequently. Reduce the heat and
gently simmer, stirring occasionally, for
15 minutes. Taste and add the remaining
sugar, if liked. Strain, if preferred, and
serve hot, or let cool and serve cold.

chile sauce

makes about 1½ cups

5 large fresh mild chiles

2 cups hot vegetable stock

1 tbsp masa harina or 1 crumbled
corn tortilla, blended with enough
water to make a thin paste

large pinch of ground cumin

1–2 garlic cloves, finely chopped

juice of 1 lime

salt

Using metal tongs, roast each chile
over an open flame until the color
darkens on all sides. Put the chiles in
a bowl and pour boiling water over
them. Cover and let cool. When the
chiles have cooled and are swollen
and soft, remove from the water with
a slotted spoon. Seed, then cut the
flesh into pieces and place in a food
processor. Process to a paste, then
mix in the hot stock.

Put the chile and stock mixture in a
pan. Add the masa harina, cumin,
garlic, and lime juice. Bring to a boil
and cook for a few minutes, stirring,
until the sauce has thickened. Adjust
the seasoning and serve.

gravy

makes about 5 cups
2 lb/900 g meat bones, raw or cooked
1 large onion, chopped
1 large carrot, chopped
2 celery stalks, chopped
1 bouquet garni
8 cups water

Preheat the oven to 400°F/200°C. Put the bones in a roasting pan and roast in the preheated oven for 20 minutes, or until browned. Remove from the oven and let cool.

Chop the bones into small pieces and put in a large pan with all the remaining ingredients. Bring to a boil, then reduce the heat, cover, and simmer for 2 hours.

Strain and leave until cold, then remove all traces of fat. Store, covered, in the refrigerator for up to 4 days. Boil vigorously for 5 minutes before using. The gravy can be frozen in ice-cube trays for up to 1 month.

satay sauce

makes about 1 cup

4 scallions, coarsely chopped

1 garlic clove, coarsely chopped

2 tsp chopped fresh ginger

6 tbsp peanut butter

1 tsp dark brown sugar

1 tsp Thai fish sauce

2 tbsp soy sauce

1 tbsp chile sauce or Tabasco sauce

1 tsp lemon juice

salt

peanuts, to garnish

Put all the ingredients into a food processor.
Add ⅔ cup of water and process to a paste.

Transfer to a pan, season with salt to taste, and heat
gently, stirring occasionally. Transfer to a bowl and
sprinkle with the peanuts. Serve warm
or cold.

mole sauce

teriyaki sauce

mole sauce

makes about 3 cups

9 mixed chiles, soaked in hot water for
  30 minutes and drained

1 onion, sliced

2–3 garlic cloves, crushed

⅔ cup sesame seeds

1 cup toasted slivered almonds

1 tsp ground coriander

4 cloves

½ tsp pepper

2–3 tbsp sunflower oil

1¼ cups chicken or vegetable stock

1 lb/450 g ripe tomatoes, peeled and chopped

2 tsp ground cinnamon

⅓ cup raisins

5 oz/140 g pumpkin seeds

2 oz/55 g dark chocolate, broken into pieces

1 tbsp red wine vinegar

Put the chiles in a food processor with the
onion, garlic, sesame seeds, almonds, coriander,
cloves, and pepper and process to form a thick
paste. Heat the oil in a pan, add the paste,
and fry for 5 minutes. Add the stock with the
tomatoes, cinnamon, raisins, and pumpkin
seeds. Bring to a boil, reduce the heat and
simmer, stirring occasionally, for 15 minutes.
Add the chocolate and vinegar to the sauce.
Cook gently for 5 minutes, then use as required.

teriyaki sauce

makes about 1 cup

1-inch/2.5-cm piece fresh ginger

1¼ cups shoyu (Japanese soy
  sauce)

3 tbsp white wine vinegar or
  cider vinegar

3 tbsp mirin (sweet rice wine)

2–3 tbsp superfine sugar

Peel and grate the ginger. Put in
a small heavy-bottom pan with
the shoyu, vinegar, mirin, and
2 tablespoons of the sugar.

Gently heat, stirring, until the
sugar has dissolved. Taste and
add the remaining sugar, if liked.
Heat gently, stirring, until the
sugar has dissolved.

Boil the mixture for 5–8 minutes,
or until reduced by half. Remove
from the heat. If you want to
use it immediately, stand the
sauce in a bowl of ice and water
for 30 minutes, or until cool.
Alternatively, let cool,
then use as required.

bread sauce

serves 6–9
1 onion
12 cloves
1 bay leaf
6 black peppercorns
2½ cups milk
2 cups fresh white breadcrumbs
2 tbsp butter
whole nutmeg, for grating
2 tbsp heavy cream (optional)
salt and pepper

Make small holes in the onion using the point of a sharp knife or a skewer, and stick the cloves in them.

Put the onion, bay leaf, and peppercorns in a pan and pour in the milk. Bring to a boil, then remove from the heat, cover, and set aside to infuse for 1 hour.

To make the sauce, discard the onion and bay leaf and strain the milk to remove the peppercorns. Return the milk to the cleaned pan and add the breadcrumbs.

Cook the sauce over very low heat for 4–5 minutes, until the breadcrumbs have swollen and the sauce is thick.

Beat in the butter and season well with salt and pepper and a good grating of nutmeg. Stir in the cream just before serving, if using.

apple sauce

makes about 2 cups

about 5 large tart cooking apples, about 2 lb/900 g
 total weight
½ cup superfine sugar
2–3 tbsp water
2 tbsp unsalted butter

Peel, core, and chop the apples. Put in a heavy-
bottom pan with the sugar and water. Bring to a boil,
then reduce the heat, cover, and simmer, stirring
occasionally, for 10–12 minutes, or until the apples
have collapsed and are fluffy.

Add the butter and stir until melted. Beat with a
wooden spoon until smooth. Serve warm or cold.

parsley sauce

makes 1½ cups
2–3 sprigs fresh parsley
2 tbsp butter, melted
¼ cup all-purpose flour
1¼ cups milk
pinch of freshly grated nutmeg
salt and pepper

Bring a small pan of water to a boil and blanch the parsley sprigs for 30 seconds. Drain, refresh under cold water, then strip off the leaves and chop finely.

Put the butter, flour, and milk into a food processor and process until smooth. Pour into a pan and bring to a boil over low heat, stirring continuously. Continue to boil, stirring continuously, for 3–4 minutes, until thickened and smooth.

Remove from the heat, stir in the parsley, and season with nutmeg and salt and pepper to taste.

dress to impress

Within these pages you will find a wide range of irresistible dressings to complement any salad, snack, or side dish to perfection.

roasted bell pepper & garlic dressing

serves 8

3 oz/85 g seeded red bell
  pepper, halved

½ tsp canola or
  vegetable oil

2 tbsp sliced garlic

1 tbsp coriander seeds

1 tsp cumin seeds

2 tsp chopped fresh rosemary

½ cup water

1 tsp sugar

¼ tsp smoked paprika

1 tbsp white wine
  vinegar

1 tbsp cornstarch,
  blended with a little
  cold water

Preheat the oven to 400°F/200°C. Put the bell pepper on a nonstick baking tray and roast in the oven until the skin blisters. Remove from the oven, let cool, then peel off the skin.

Heat the oil in a small pan over medium heat, add the garlic, and cook, stirring continuously, until golden brown. Add the coriander seeds and cumin seeds and cook for 1 minute, stirring. Add the rosemary, water, sugar, paprika, and vinegar and bring to a boil. Gradually add the cornstarch, stirring continuously, and cook until thickened.

Add the roasted bell pepper, put the mixture in a food processor, and process until smooth. Pass through a fine strainer, cover with plastic wrap to prevent a skin from forming, and let cool.

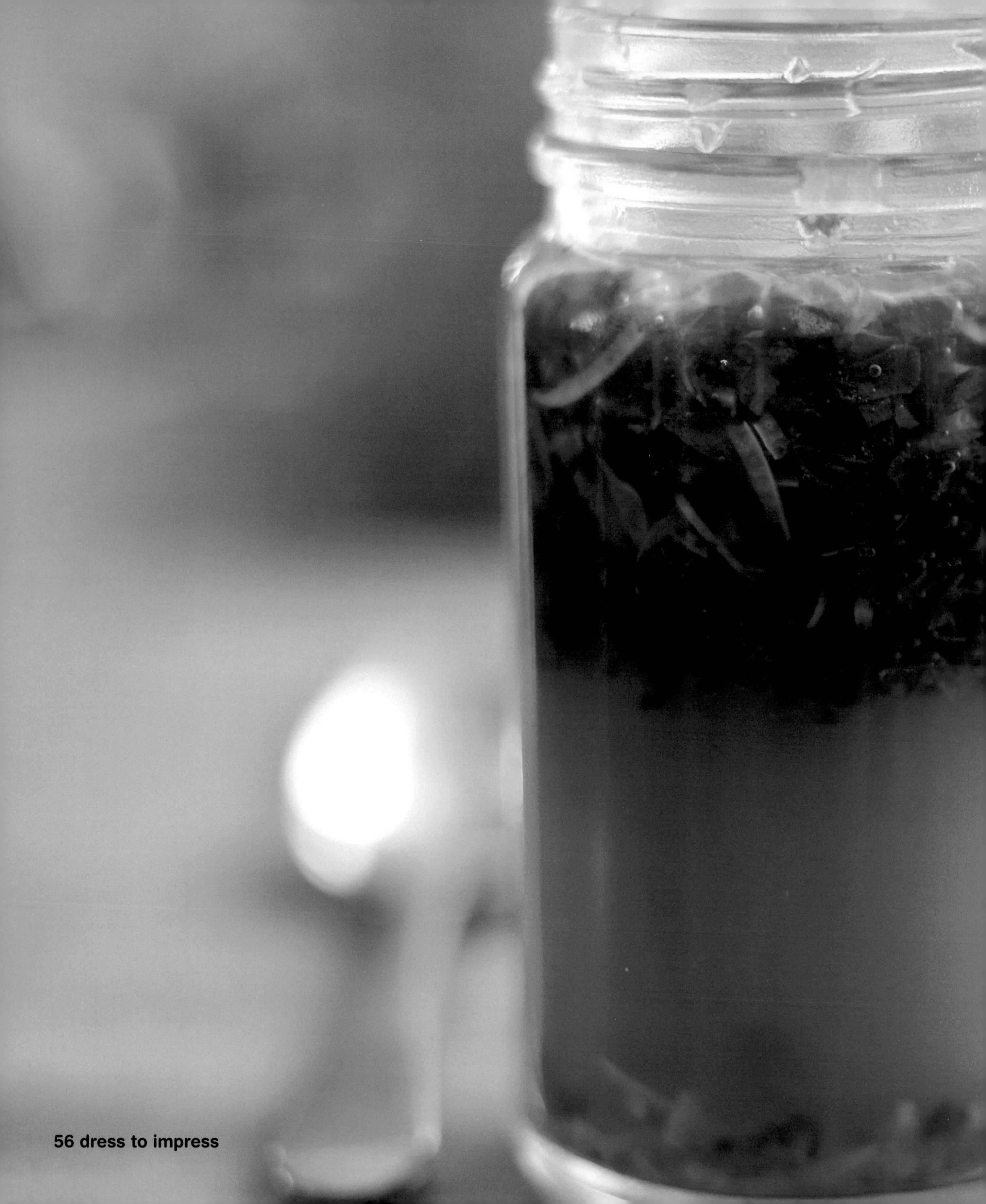

basil, chive & lemon dressing

serves 4–6

1–1½ lb/450–675 g small potatoes, skins on
5 cooked artichoke hearts
2 oz/55 g chopped dill pickle
1 tbsp fresh dill, chopped
20 chives, snipped
4 tbsp basil, chive, and lemon vinegar
1 tsp Dijon mustard
2 tbsp olive oil
1 tbsp fresh lemon juice
salt and pepper

Bring a large pan of lightly salted water to a boil, add the potatoes, and cook until soft. Cut into bite-size pieces. Cut the artichoke hearts into bite-size pieces and combine in a mixing bowl with the potatoes. Add the pickle, dill, and chives.

Whisk together the vinegar, mustard, oil, and lemon juice. Season with salt and pepper to taste. Pour over the potato and artichoke mixture and mix.

Serve immediately or store, covered, in the refrigerator and bring to room temperature before serving.

pink grapefruit, raspberry, wasabi & sesame oil dressing

serves 12

1 pink grapefruit, halved

⅓ cup water

1 tbsp white wine vinegar

1 tsp sugar

1 tbsp cornstarch, blended with a little cold water

¼ cup raspberries

¼ tsp wasabi paste

1 tsp sesame oil

Working over a bowl, cut out the grapefruit segments between the membranes. Reserve a third of the segments and squeeze a generous ⅓ cup of the juice from the remainder.

Put the grapefruit juice, water, vinegar, and sugar into a small pan over medium heat and bring to a boil. Gradually add the cornstarch mixture, stirring, cook until thick, then remove from the heat. Add the grapefruit, raspberries, wasabi paste, and oil.

Put the mixture into a food processor and process until smooth. Pass through a fine strainer. Cover with plastic wrap and chill in the refrigerator. Keep the dressing in the refrigerator until ready to use.

slim-line dressing

tomato dressing

slim-line dressing

serves 4

1¼ cups low-fat plain
  yogurt
1 tsp English mustard
2–3 tbsp lemon juice
4 tsp sunflower oil
salt and pepper

Put all the ingredients into a
food processor, season with salt
and pepper to taste, and process
on medium speed until
thoroughly combined.

tomato dressing

serves 2–4

2 tbsp balsamic vinegar, or red
  or white wine vinegar
4–6 tbsp extra virgin olive oil
1 tsp Dijon mustard
pinch of superfine sugar
1 tbsp torn fresh basil leaves
1 tbsp chopped sun-dried tomatoes
salt and pepper

Place all the ingredients in a
screw-top jar, secure the top, and
shake well. Alternatively, beat all
the ingredients together in a small
bowl. Use as much oil as you like.

If you only have salad leaves to
dress, 4 tablespoons of oil will be
sufficient, but if you have heavier
ingredients such as potatoes, you
will need about 6 tablespoons
of oil.

Use the dressing immediately. If
you want to store it, do not add the
herbs—it will then keep for 3–4
days in the refrigerator.

green dressing

serves 4

1¼ cups low-fat plain yogurt

2 tsp Dijon mustard

2–3 tbsp white wine vinegar

4 tsp sunflower oil

2 tbsp coarsely chopped fresh parsley

2 tbsp snipped fresh chives

2 tbsp coarsely chopped fresh tarragon

1 scallion, coarsely chopped

1 tbsp coarsely chopped watercress

salt and pepper

Put the yogurt, mustard, vinegar, and oil into a food processor and season with salt and pepper to taste. Process on medium speed until thoroughly combined. Add the parsley, chives, tarragon, scallion, and watercress and process for a few seconds to chop finely and blend.

garlic, chile & oregano oil

makes about 1 cup

5 garlic cloves, halved lengthwise

2 tbsp seeded and chopped red hot chile

1 tsp dried oregano

1 cup canola oil

Preheat the oven to 300°F/150°C. Combine the garlic, chile, and oregano with the oil in an ovenproof glass measuring cup. Place on a glass pie plate in the center of the oven and heat for 1½–2 hours. The temperature of the oil should reach 250°F/120°C.

Remove from the oven, let cool, then strain through cheesecloth into a clean jar. Store, covered, in the refrigerator. Alternatively, leave the garlic and chile pieces in the oil and strain before using.

sweet & sour dressing

honey & yogurt dressing

sweet & sour dressing

serves 2–4

2 tbsp lemon juice, or red or white
   wine vinegar
4–6 tbsp extra virgin olive oil
1 tsp Dijon mustard
pinch of superfine sugar
1 tbsp honey
1 tsp finely grated fresh ginger
1 tbsp toasted sesame seeds
1 tbsp freshly chopped parsley
salt and pepper

Place all the ingredients in a
screw-top jar, secure the top, and
shake well. Alternatively, beat all
the ingredients together in a small
bowl.

A dressing for salad leaves will
require 4 tablespoons of oil, but
heavier ingredients, such as
potatoes, will require about
6 tablespoons of oil.

honey & yogurt dressing

makes about ½ cup

1 tbsp clear honey
⅓ cup lowfat plain yogurt
salt and pepper

Put the honey and yogurt in
a glass bowl and beat with a
fork until thoroughly combined.
Season with salt and pepper to
taste.

dill & peppercorn vinegar

makes about 1 cup

1 cup cider vinegar

6 sprigs fresh dill

1 tsp whole black peppercorns

Put the vinegar in a pan over medium heat and bring to a boil. Reduce the heat and simmer for 2 minutes. Add the dill and peppercorns, turn off the heat, and let stand for several minutes until cool.

Pour into a clean jar, seal, and refrigerate or keep in a dark place until ready to use.

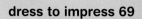
dress to impress 69

garlic vinaigrette

makes about ⅔ cup

½ cup garlic-flavored olive oil

3 tbsp white wine vinegar or lemon juice

1–2 garlic cloves, crushed

1 tsp Dijon mustard

½ tsp superfine sugar

salt and pepper

Put all the ingredients in a screw-top jar, secure the lid, and shake vigorously until an emulsion forms. Taste and adjust the seasoning if necessary.

Use at once or store in an airtight container in the refrigerator for up to a month. Remove the garlic cloves after 1 week. Always whisk or shake the dressing before using.

herb vinaigrette

makes about ⅔ cup

½ cup olive or other vegetable oil
3 tbsp white wine vinegar or lemon juice
1½ tbsp chopped fresh herbs, such as chives, parsley, or mint
1 tsp Dijon mustard
½ tsp superfine sugar
salt and pepper

Put all the ingredients in a screw-top jar, secure the lid, and shake vigorously until a thick emulsion forms. Taste and adjust the seasoning if necessary.

Use immediately or store in an airtight container in the refrigerator for up to 3 days. Always whisk or shake the dressing before using, and strain through a fine nonmetallic strainer if the herbs begin to darken.

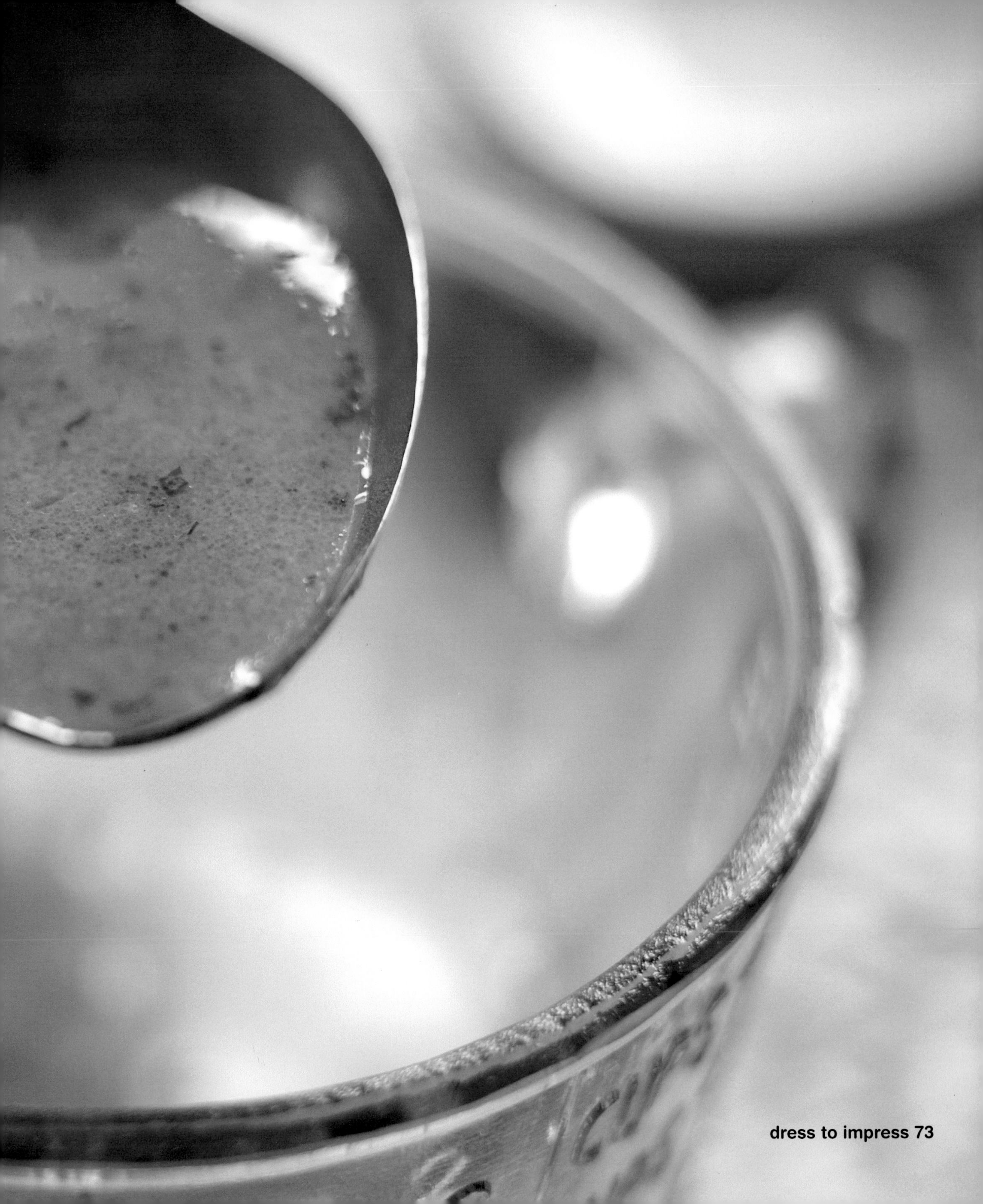

sweet eats

When it comes to dessert, what could be better than a sweet sauce? You will find the wonderful sauces in this chapter impossible to resist.

chocolate fudge sauce

makes about ⅔ cup

⅔ cup heavy cream

4 tbsp unsalted butter, cut into small pieces

3 tbsp superfine sugar

6 oz/175 g white chocolate, broken into pieces

2 tbsp brandy

Pour the cream into the top of a double boiler or a heatproof bowl set over a pan of gently simmering water. Add the butter and sugar and stir until the mixture is smooth. Remove from the heat.

Stir in the chocolate, a few pieces at a time, waiting until each batch has melted before adding the next. Add the brandy and stir the sauce until smooth. Cool to room temperature before serving.

nutty butterscotch sauce

serves 4

1⅔ cups light brown sugar
½ cup water
1 tbsp rum
6 tbsp unsalted butter
½ cup heavy cream, gently warmed
⅔ cup peanuts, chopped

Put the sugar and water into a heavy-bottom pan, place over medium heat, and stir until the sugar has dissolved. Bring to a boil, then let bubble for 6–7 minutes. Stir in the rum and cook for another minute.

Using oven mitts, remove from the heat and carefully stir in the butter until melted. Gradually stir in the cream until the mixture is smooth. Finally, stir in the nuts.

custard sauce

makes about 2½ cups
3 tbsp cornstarch
2½ cups milk
¼ cup sugar
2 tbsp unsalted butter
1 egg
½ tsp vanilla extract

Put the cornstarch into a bowl with 3 tablespoons of the milk. Stir to a paste. Put the remaining milk in a pan and bring just to a boil.

Meanwhile, put the sugar, butter, egg, and vanilla extract into a food processor and process until smooth.

Pour the hot milk into the cornstarch mixture, stirring continuously. Return to the pan and cook over low heat, stirring continuously, for 2 minutes, or until thick. With the motor running, pour the hot cornstarch mixture into a food processor and process until well combined with the sugar mixture. Pour into a pitcher and serve immediately.

french chocolate sauce

chocolate brandy sauce

french chocolate sauce

makes ⅔ cup

⅓ cup heavy cream

3 oz/85 g dark chocolate,
  broken into small pieces

2 tbsp orange liqueur

Bring the cream gently to a boil
in a small heavy-bottom pan
over low heat. Remove the pan
from the heat, add the broken
chocolate, and stir until smooth.

Stir in the liqueur and serve
immediately, or keep the sauce
warm until required.

chocolate brandy sauce

serves 4

9 oz/250 g dark chocolate
  (must contain at least
  50 percent cocoa solids)

½ cup heavy cream

2 tbsp brandy

Break or chop the chocolate
into small pieces and place in
the top of a double boiler or in
a heatproof bowl set over a pan
of simmering water. Pour in the
cream and stir until melted and
smooth. Stir in the brandy, pour
into a pitcher, and serve.

mocha sauce

serves 6

⅔ cup heavy cream
½ cup unsalted butter
¼ cup light brown sugar
6 oz/175 g dark chocolate, broken into pieces
1 tbsp instant coffee granules
2 tbsp dark rum (optional)

Pour the cream into a heatproof bowl and add the butter and sugar. Set over a pan of gently simmering water and cook, stirring continuously, until smooth. Remove from the heat and set aside to cool slightly.

Stir in the chocolate and coffee granules, continue stirring until it has melted. Stir in the rum, if using, then let the sauce cool to room temperature before serving.

vanilla toffee sauce

serves 4

½ cup plus 1 tbsp butter

2 cups light brown sugar

1 cup dark corn syrup

2 tbsp maple syrup

2 tbsp water

14 fl oz/400 ml canned sweetened condensed milk

1 tsp vanilla extract

½ tsp ground cinnamon

1 tbsp rum

Put the butter into a heatproof bowl set over a pan of simmering water and melt gently. Add the sugar, corn syrup, maple syrup, water, condensed milk, vanilla extract, and cinnamon. Stir until thick and smooth, then stir in the rum and cook for another minute. Remove from the heat, carefully pour the mixture into a pitcher, and serve.

berry sauce

orange sauce

berry sauce

serves 6

8 oz/225 g berries, such as
  blackberries or raspberries
2 tbsp water
2–3 tbsp superfine sugar
2 tbsp fruit liqueur, such as
  crème de cassis or crème de
  framboise

Put all the ingredients into a
small, heavy-bottom pan and
heat gently, until the sugar
has dissolved and the fruit
juices run. Process to a paste
in a food processor, then push
through a nonmetallic strainer
into a serving bowl to remove
the seeds. Add more sugar if
necessary and serve warm or
cold.

orange sauce

serves 4

¼ cup superfine sugar
1 tbsp water
finely grated rind of 1 large
  orange
½ cup freshly squeezed orange
  juice
4 tbsp unsalted butter, diced
1 tbsp orange liqueur

Place the sugar in a wide sauté
pan or skillet over medium
heat and stir in the water.
Continue stirring until the sugar
dissolves, then increase the
heat to high and leave the syrup
to bubble for 1–2 minutes, until
it just begins to turn golden
brown.

Stir in the orange rind and
juice, then add the butter and
continue stirring until it melts.
Stir in the orange liqueur,
remove from the heat, and serve
warm.

fruit coulis

makes about 1¼ cups

peach coulis

1 lb/450 g peaches

1 tbsp lemon juice

2 tbsp superfine sugar

2 tbsp Amaretto liqueur

melba sauce

1 lb/450 g raspberries

1 tbsp lemon juice

3 tbsp superfine
sugar

tropical fruit coulis

1 mango

1 papaya

3 kiwis

2 tbsp superfine sugar

3 tbsp white rum

To make the Peach Coulis, using a sharp knife, cut a cross in the base of each peach, then plunge into boiling water for 15–30 seconds. Drain and refresh in iced water. Peel off the skins, halve the peaches and remove the pits, then slice coarsely. Put the peaches, lemon juice, and sugar into a food processor. Process to a smooth paste, scraping down the sides as necessary. Transfer to a bowl and stir in the liqueur. Cover and chill for 1 hour.

For the Melba Sauce, put the fruit, lemon juice, and sugar into a food processor. Process to a smooth paste, scraping down the sides as necessary, then rub through a nonmetallic strainer into a bowl to remove the seeds. Cover and chill for 1 hour.

For the Tropical Fruit Coulis, pit the mango and put the flesh into a food processor. Cut the papaya in half lengthwise and scoop out the seeds with a spoon. Scoop out any fibers. Discard the seeds and fibers. Scoop out the flesh, chop coarsely, and add to the food processor. Slice the kiwis and add to the food processor with the sugar. Process to a paste, scraping down the sides as necessary, then rub through a nonmetallic strainer into a bowl. Stir in the rum. Cover and chill for 1 hour before serving.

maple sauce

serves 4

¾ cup maple syrup

4 tbsp butter

½ tsp ground allspice

Put all the ingredients into a pan over medium heat. Bring to a boil, stirring, then reduce the heat and simmer for 3 minutes.

chile pineapple sauce

serves 6

2 tbsp olive oil

2 onions, chopped

8 oz/225 g fresh pineapple, chopped

1 tsp ground cinnamon

1 tbsp white wine vinegar

½–1 tsp chile powder

salt

Heat the oil in a heavy-based frying pan. Add the onions and pineapple and cook over a low heat, stirring occasionally, for 10 minutes, or until golden.

Using a slotted spoon, and draining off as much oil as possible, transfer the onion and pineapple mixture to a food processor. Add the cinnamon and vinegar and chile powder to taste, then season to taste with salt. Process until smooth.

Transfer to a serving dish, cover tightly with plastic wrap, and chill in the refrigerator until required.

almonds 45
amaretto liqueur 90
apple sauce 48
apples, cooking 48
arrabbiata sauce 15
artichoke hearts 57
asparagus 26
asparagus sauce 26

bacon 12
barbecue sauce 39
basil, chive & lemon
    dressing 57
basil pesto 23
béarnaise sauce 17
béchamel sauce 17
beef 12
bell peppers
    green 24
    red 54
berries 58, 89, 90
berry sauce 89
black bean sauce 18
black beans 18
bolognese sauce classic 12
brandy 76, 83
bread sauce 46
butterscotch sauce nutty 78

carrots 12, 17, 24, 40
celery 10, 12, 40
chicken livers 12
chile pineapple sauce 94
chile sauce 39
chiles 15, 18, 39 45, 64
chocolate 45, 76, 83, 84
chocolate brandy sauce 83
chocolate fudge sauce 76
chocolate sauce french 83
cointreau 32
condensed milk sweetened 86
corn syrup 86
cranberries 32
cranberry sauce 32
custard sauce 80

dill & peppercorn vinegar 68
dill pickle 57

eggs 20, 80

fruit liqueur 32, 83, 89

garlic, chile & oregano oil 64

garlic vinaigrette 71
ginger, fresh 18, 24, 42, 45, 67
grapefruit, pink 58
gravy 28, 40
green dressing 62

herb vinaigrette 72
hollandaise sauce 20
honey 67
honey & yogurt dressing 67
horseradish sauce 34

kiwis 90

lemon juice 18, 20, 23, 42, 57, 61,
    67, 90
lime juice 39

mangoes 90
maple sauce 92
maple syrup 86, 92
masa harina 39
melba sauce 90
mint sauce 36
mirin 45
mocha sauce 84
mole sauce 45
mushrooms 12, 26
mustard
    dijon 57, 61, 62, 67, 71, 72
    english 61
    powdered 39

orange juice 32, 89
orange liqueur 32, 83, 89
orange sauce 89

papayas 90
parmesan cheese 12, 23
parsley sauce 50
peach coulis 90
peanut butter 42
peanuts 42, 78
pine nuts 23
pineapples 24
pink grapefruit, raspberry, wasabi
    & sesame oil dressing 58
potatoes 57
pumpkin seeds 45

raisins 45
raspberries 58, 90
red currant jelly 28
red wine sauce 28

roasted bell pepper & garlic
    dressing 54
rum 78, 84, 86, 90

satay sauce 42
scallions 18, 26, 42, 62
sesame seeds 45, 67
shallots 17, 18
shoyu 45
slim-line dressing 61
soy sauce 18, 24, 42, 45
spaghetti 12
sun-dried tomato pesto 23
sweet & sour dressing 67
sweet & sour sauce 24

teriyaki sauce 45
thai fish sauce 42
tomato dressing 61
tomato ketchup 24
tomato paste 10, 12, 15, 39
tomato sauce fresh 10
tomatoes 10, 15, 45
tropical fruit coulis 90

vanilla toffee sauce 86

wasabi paste 58
watercress 62
wine
    red 28
    sweet rice 45
    white 12, 36
worcestershire sauce 39

yogurt 61, 62, 67